It's How You

~Finish~

Troy Taylor

Visit us on the web at:

www.troydtaylor.com

I would first like to thank my Heavenly Father for allowing me to author my first book and for providing me with every lesson shared here. What an awesome God we serve.

I would like to dedicate this book to all of my children; My three handsome sons Troy Jr, Trevor and Trevon and my beautiful daughter Monica. Daddy loves you more than you'll ever know. To everyone who became a part of my story, good or not so good, to you I say thank you. Thank you for being what I needed in each season.

To my mommy, I say thank you for life and love. Thank you for showing me what strength looks like. To my siblings Aaron and Kytrina, I love you!

To my best friends, Earl, Jennifer and Courtney I love you so dearly. Your friendship means the world to me and has carried me through many storms. And to my spiritual father Dr. Hayward Cordy for encouraging me to write this book. Thank you for always believing in me. Love you dad!

To everyone who has played a significant role in my life I say thank you! To all of my family and friends I send my love.

Dr. Hayward Cordy

DREAMS

by

Langston Hughes

Hold fast to dreams
For if dreams die
Life is a broken-winged bird
That Cannot fly.

Hold fast to dreams
For when dreams go
Life is a barren field
Frozen with snow.

In his poem, DREAMS, Langston Hughes, poet laureate of Harlem during the Harlem Renaissance, admonishes us to 'hold fast' to our dreams, our dreams about our future, the things we hope for and the goals that we want to achieve. In describing a life without dreams as being like a 'broken-winged bird that cannot fly,' Hughes reminds us that dreams give our lives purpose and meaning, and without them, life is harsh and difficult. Hughes equates the loss of dreams to living in a cold and barren field, a place with no joy, no life, and no hope.

Troy Taylor's life epitomizes the story of a broken-winged bird living in a cold field filled with abject poverty, isolation, low self-esteem, emotional abuse, and rejection. Troy held on to his dreams and has succeeded in spite of the obstacles that he faced in life. Rather than being dissuaded by his fears and struggles, during his deepest times of despair, Troy held fast to his faith and his dreams.

In my 2015 autobiography, *Damaged Goods: Lessons Learned In Poverty Applied To Life,* I shared an email that I received from Troy after having no contact with him for almost nine years. Troy and I met when he was in middle school after he was assigned to an alternative education program where I served as Director. He was with me for approximately two years before he transitioned back to his home school in Jefferson County. I did not hear from Troy for several years but kept up with his progress. In 2007, while serving as Superintendent of Schools in Wrightsville, Georgia, I was pleasantly surprised to have received an email from Troy. Troy updated me as to his life experiences since the last time that we had talked.

Troy's story and life experiences encompass all of the societal, cultural, educational, and environmental factors that negatively impact the lives of the majority of Black males in America, leaving many with no hope, no future, no dreams. Despite having so many negative lived experiences that often lead children toward a trajectory of self-destruction and hopelessness, Troy remained optimistic and goal oriented and has succeeded despite the odds.

Troy, like many black males and children of poverty often do, worked very hard to hide and mask signs of his negative lived experiences including poverty growing up. In his autobiography, *It's How You Finish*, Troy is transparent and reveals his successes, failures, struggles, pain, and dreams in order to encourage others who struggle and don't quite fit in to hold to their dreams and never give up realizing that it is not where or how we begin but *It's How You Finish.*

When I read Troy's life story, I see many parallels between his life and mine. He learned as I did that God cannot heal what we are afraid to reveal and to see himself as God sees him rather than allow others to determine his future and his identity.

You will enjoy reading this book and you will be inspired, as I am, by the story of a genuinely outstanding young man who came to know himself, and his capabilities and refused to let the hurtful words or actions reflected in the insecurities of others define him.

With great admiration and respect for my son, Troy Taylor

Hayward Cordy Ed. D
Author
Executive Director
Oconee RESA
2018-19 State President
Professional Association of Georgia Educators

CONTENTS

CHAPTER 1:   SUCH A BAD LITTLE BOY   **6**

CHAPTER 2:   WHO AM I (THEN AND NOW)   **22**

CHAPTER 3:   THE FATHER I NEVER HAD   **33**

CHAPTER 4:   SEARCHING FOR MY PLACE   **38**

CHAPTER 5:   THE GREAT ESCAPE   **47**

CHAPTER 6:   ADVENTURES OF A DETERMINED FATHER   **61**

CHAPTER 7:   A TRUE TEST OF MY FAITH   **77**

CHAPTER 8:   I SAID I DO THEN DIDN'T   **98**

CHAPTER 9:   THE INTROVERT   **111**

CHAPTER 10:   NO SEAT AT THE PRESIDENTS TABLE   **114**

CHAPTER 11:   WHAT I'VE LEARNED   **122**

It's How You

~Finish~

———————————————————

CHAPTER ONE

"You are altogether beautiful,
my love; there is no flaw in you." *Song of Solomon*
4:7 (ESV)

~Such a Bad Little Boy~

"You know you were such a bad little boy," many have said and still say to this day with laughter in their voices. They continue, "But I'm so proud of you now," as if I should take this as something akin to a compliment.

As far back as I can remember, I was always a deep thinker. I'd often find myself wrapped up in a frenzy of curiosity, fantasy and imagination. I always knew I was slightly different from many of the people and children around me. As a young boy, this was very challenging because I didn't understand what set me apart from others. I didn't know what caused this, yet I knew that I was singular.

When I was about eight, I became close friends with the son of my then pastor, a stereotypical preacher's kid (PK). All the young girls in the church ran after him, and I envied his charisma. He was also a musician in the church. One day at a tent revival, there was no drum player. I had never played the drums before, but I felt like I could. I'm not sure why, but I did. I had always loved rhythms and beating on my mom's pots and pans to make my own music. At this tent revival, I had my opportunity. I mustered up the courage to walk my eight-year-old self-up to the drums, sit down and just start playing. I went on to play the drums for my church for the next thirteen years.

My greatest mentor at the time was the PK with all the charisma. Little by little he showed me new things about the drums and how to play them. Before long we were a duo. Everywhere he went, I was stuck to his side. He was my best friend in the whole world, the big brother I never had. When I was alone, I felt the weight of being an outcast, but when I was with my big brother, I knew I belonged. However, one day we had a pretty heated disagreement. He and I had not seen eye to eye on many other things; he was about seven years older for goodness' sake. But this time was different. I was about thirteen and had shown up at his apartment after school. One thing led to another, and he kicked me out of his home. As I was leaving, we exchanged words once more, and he even pushed me. I walked about a half mile home in tears. Of course, we saw each other after that, but our friendship and brotherhood would never be the same. Outside of my biological father, this was my first experience with rejection by a male figure that I greatly admired. I never forgot that moment. Dr. Maya Angelou said, "People may forget what you did, or even forget what you said, but they never forget how you made them feel."

Growing up without a father consistently present, due to him being in and out of prison on drug and theft charges, was very difficult. Because women surrounded me, at times I took on their characteristics and mannerisms. I never learned to play sports (thus I never developed an interest in them even as an adult) or do any of the things most young boys do and learn through their teen years, but I always wanted to. I always wanted to fit in somewhere. Anywhere. But I never did. No matter how much I tried, I never did. I remember my mom putting me into recreational basketball. I remember thinking to myself that if I can learn this sport and play it well, maybe the other kids would accept me and love me. We all want to be loved. So, I went to every practice hoping to gain the skills needed to be a great athlete. However, during one of our first games, the coach reluctantly put me in the game. (Side note: Adults, be careful how you interact with kids. If you reject them, it can hurt just as much as, if not more, than rejection by their peers.)

The buzzer rang, and I was in the game. I remember running out onto the court thinking that I still had no clue what I was doing, as the coach hadn't really "coached" me.

He and other coaches tended to work with the kids who already had a certain level of talent. I ran down the court, wide open for a pass. My teammate threw me the ball, and I was on...except I didn't know how to dribble or shoot! In an attempt to do something, anything, I threw the ball in the direction of the goal. It seemed like I threw it from nearly half a court away. Needless to say, it went over the goal and out of bounds. Everyone laughed, and the coach immediately took me out of the game. I was humiliated, and sat in the back of the van on the way home. I listened to the other kids commend each other for jobs well done; however, I did not speak. Once again, I retreated into my safe place, into my mind and thoughts. I don't recall returning to any other practices or games after that.

Later in life, I questioned whether or not it would have been different for me if I had had a father. Oh, how I longed for a father. Someone to teach me how to dribble a ball. How to shoot a ball. How to interact with the other boys around me. How to walk and talk like the stereotypical man. I didn't want to stand out. I didn't want to be different. What I wanted was to blend into my surroundings and never be noticed. That's what I longed for. To be invisible.

Even as a child my sexuality seemed always to be called into question. A single mother raised me. I had an older sister, and my younger brother was born when I was nine. I remember even in elementary school being called "faggot" by family, other kids and adults. At the time, I wasn't sure what a faggot was, but I knew it was something bad. I was unaware of my feminine mannerisms because they were normal to me. I didn't see what I was doing to provoke this name calling. I once heard Bishop T.D Jakes of The Potter's House say, "You can see all but one thing in a room; yourself."

I recall this one time when I was in the third grade, I went into the bathroom to use it like the rest of the kids during our restroom break. I was relatively introverted, so I would always use closed stalls even if there were urinals available. I walked over to the first stall and opened the door to go in, when I realized that someone was already in it. I quickly excused myself, but at that very second some other young men walked into the bathroom and said something like, "Eww, they're gay!" I tried to explain what happened, but naturally, no one listened or cared. That was the beginning of many years of being called gay and a faggot. That reference wouldn't subside until I was in high school. I believe it was while returning to class that same day in elementary school that my male teacher got wind of what had happened in the bathroom.

As we filed into class, he stood in the doorway, and as I approached, he waved at me with a limp wrist, and in an exaggerated, effeminate voice said, "Heeeeey, Trooooy." I was devastated and extremely embarrassed. I didn't understand why my teacher, of all people, felt the need to humiliate me on top of what my peers already had done. I cried my eyes out to my mother, and she contacted the school immediately, but unfortunately nothing was done.

I continued to ask myself why it seemed that no matter what I did, no one ever liked or accepted me. I began to resign myself to the rejections and created ways to reject others before they rejected me. Even as a child, I've always had a certain level of pride and never wanted anyone to see me sweat.

One time in fourth grade I thought I could buy friendship. I went to school with ten one-dollar bills in my pocket. At that time, towards the end of the school day, we were allowed to go to the cafeteria to buy a small ice cream for about fifty cents. Somehow one of my classmates knew that I had a few dollars and asked for one to buy some ice cream. I thought that maybe if I did this, I'd gain a new friend. So, I gave him one of my dollars. The others saw that, and all started asking me for a dollar. I couldn't believe that they all were talking to me and seemed to like me (at least at that moment). In my mind, here was my chance to acquire new friends. I ended up giving away all of my money and I didn't even have enough left to buy myself some ice cream. Needless to say, not one of these kids was interested in friendship after the money and ice cream were gone. I learned that very day that you can't buy genuine love or friendship.

So, as I got older, I grew more and more isolated and lonely. My home life was difficult at times, too. We lived well below the poverty line, and during much of my childhood I slept on the floor. I remember when the government distributed powered milk and canned meats to people on welfare. Boy, that was nasty stuff, but it was all we had at the time.

During the winter months we all had to stay sealed in our rooms as we had no heat throughout the house. We'd stuff clothes and blankets around the bottoms of the doors to prevent the heat from seeping out. To go to the kitchen was an ordeal all in itself. We had to wear a coat and hat because sometimes the air outside of our rooms was colder than it was outside the house, in fact so cold that liquid items froze if left on the kitchen counter.

Our plumbing malfunctioned, too. When we flushed the toilet it no longer drained into the septic tank under the house but went under the adjacent wall and into the hall on the other side. You can imagine that our house smelled like sewage, and in the winter months that sewage froze into the hallway carpet.

Rats and roaches were common house guests. You learn from years of living with them never to leave certain items out of the cabinet. If you did, they would be partially eaten by the next morning. You learn to put almost everything in the refrigerator for safe keeping. You also learn to wait a few moments before turning on the kitchen light or walking into the kitchen, to give the roaches time to clear the kitchen floor and run back into their hiding places.

Many nights my sister matter-of-factly shared with me that she saw mice and roaches in the bed with me as she passed by on her way to the bathroom. I suppose they needed to keep warm, too. I'll never forget when I was about nine years old, I had the scare of a lifetime. I was lying in my mother's bed and heard a relatively loud movement under the bed. This wasn't uncommon for us as we were used to mice running around the house and making noise. However, this time the movement was louder than what a typical little mouse could make. With my nine-year-old wisdom I decided to be as quiet as possible to see if this thing would come out, so I could catch a glimpse of it. I slowly peeked my head over the side of the bed and out came a huge rat! I jumped and screamed, and the rat ran out from under the bed and down the hall. It was so big it actually struggled to run! I followed it for a moment, then watched it slip into a cutout under the cabinet, never to be seen again. I assume the way it left was the way it came in. That was traumatizing to say the least.

My mother tried her best to provide what she could by working a minimum-wage job at a local shirt factory. She and my father had been married to each other twice. Unfortunately, my father was addicted to illegal drugs, so she divorced him twice.

Later in life, as an adult sitting at the bedside of my dying grandmother, I was able to ask my dad how he could have had three children and not be present in any of their lives. I wondered what it was about drugs that made him willing to give up his entire family for them. He told me the narcotics were so powerful, that you somehow know you will regret what you are about to do, but you do it anyway. All I could say was, "Wow."

I've never harbored resentment toward my father. Many people can't understand that, but I've always felt compassion for him. He was merely a broken man. He was also a man greatly rejected by his father, and at times mistreated by his mother. I believe he turned to drugs as a means of escape from a lifetime of rejection.

My older sister, contrary to popular belief, has a heart of gold. However, all of my life she seemed to hate me. I didn't know why that was when I was a child, and I still don't understand it to this day, but I love her. Many days I'd come home from one of my usually miserable days at school only to have my very own sister call me the same names my peers called me, faggot. So, when I say my sister has a heart of gold, I mean that in spite of her outwardly hateful behavior to me and many others around her, she is actually one of the most generous people I know.

As I got older, I learned my sister suffered from her own emotional issues, so I learned not to take to heart her behavior toward me and the things she said. But as a child, boy did it hurt. My mom once shared with me that the day they brought me home from the hospital, my sister looked at me in the crib and frowned. It sounds comical now, but I can picture that happening. And my little brother and I never really developed a deep bond partly because of our nine-year age difference, and because I wasn't around the house very much. I was always into something related to church and music. By age eleven, I had taught myself to play not only the drums but also the piano and to sing. Boy did I love to sing! In fact, my sister and I became known around our little city for our singing and ability to harmonize really tightly with each other in spite of our relationship issues.

I knew from a young age that we were very poor. My first paying job at age eleven was at Mr. Billy Weeks' auto parts store in Wadley, Georgia. When I walked in and told him I was looking for a job, Mr. Weeks laughed and said, "How old are you?" When I told him, he laughed again and said he'd give me a job, but he'd have to talk to my mom about it first. I wanted the autonomy to be able to buy my school clothes and supplies since I knew my mother struggled to afford those things. Even though she was married to my dad at that time, he was rarely around, continuously in and out of prison on drug and theft charges.

My father was a very talented man and could do anything with his hands. He was great at electrical work and was also a skilled artist. He painted and drew things that amazed me. I inherited some of his talents. However, when my dad was home, I was terrified of him. He didn't speak to me much, and when he did, he usually yelled. He and my mom spent day and night in shouting matches. My siblings and I stayed in our rooms listening to them fuss and argue, hoping that dad would leave and never return. There was never any peace in the house when he was there, especially when he wanted to get high.

Being the oldest and a boy, I felt he took a lot of his frustration out on me. My dad didn't hit women, so he never touched mom or my older sister. And my brother was too little to be dad's target, so that left me. One day, after returning home from church, my dad noticed that the living room window was left slightly open. The apartment we were living in had one bedroom and a study. My mom and dad slept in the bedroom, and my sister and little brother slept in the converted study. I slept on the floor in the living room. The night before it must have been warm, so I opened the window for air and forgot to close it when we left for church the next morning. I don't know what triggered my dad, but he went ballistic on me. He grabbed me by the shirt and threw me against the wall with one hand while drawing back his other fist. I remember thinking, if he hits me, he'll break my face. My mom ran up behind him screaming, waving an iron in the air and saying, "If you hit my son, I'll bust your head with this iron!" Thank God he didn't punch me that day.

Chapter Thought: No one will ever see value in you if you don't recognize it first. There is nothing wrong with you. You were created exactly the way God wanted you to be regardless of what others think. You were given every single tool you'd ever need in life even if you haven't had the chance to pull them out of the tool box just yet. They're in there! And guess what, you are NEVER left to do this work alone! Even in the darkest moments of your life, when you feel thrown against a metaphorical wall, I promise God is with you and preparing you for "greater" things. He's simply teaching you to walk, not by what you see, but by what you don't see, that is, by having faith. Without faith it's impossible to please Him! Do you believe that? I'm convinced that all things work together for the good of those who love the Lord and those who are called according to His purpose! Hang in there! Push forward to see what lies ahead in YOUR next chapter! I'm excited for you and the changing of seasons in your life!

CHAPTER TWO

"We know that our old man was crucified with Him
so that the body of sin would no longer dominate us,
so that we would no longer be enslaved to sin."
Romans 6:6 (NET)

~Who Am I? Then and Now~

When I was in kindergarten, my mother moved us from a tiny town called Bartow Georgia, to the "big city" of Macon, Georgia. She found a church for us, and she quickly made friends with a few folks. Some of these people helped my mom out by babysitting us when she had to work. At that time, my mother was a radio host for a station called 99 Ways. One particular friend that my mom allowed to watch us was a charming female minister in the church. She had three kids herself, all of which were older than my sister and I.

One evening, one of her sons, "Mike," wanted to play this touching game under his bed. Being a little boy, I didn't see any harm in it. We went under the bed and he started touching me. I thought it was bizarre but figured it was just a game. Periodically, he'd leave me under the bed to go out and check to see if anyone was coming or looking for us. I unwittingly stayed under the bed even while people were coming in and out of the room. No one knew I was there but Mike. These interactions were my first encounters with sexuality, and it had a profound impact on me as I can still recall it today. That young man's mother passed away when he was a bit older, and he went on to become the "Bishop" of his own church. I never saw him in person again.

In order to have some help with my siblings and me, my mom later moved us back to our small hometown and we bid Macon, Georgia farewell. As a young boy, I was very curious about everything around me, and still had residual effects in my mind, from those encounters with Mike. I always wanted to know random bits of information, like what astronauts ate in space or how grapes turned to raisins, as well as things that pertained to me and my existence.

I remember when America Online, or AOL, began in the early '90s, they sent out free software and subscriptions through the mail. Dial-up was everything! However, given my very vivid imagination, and with little to no guidance, I found myself engulfed in an online fantasy world of pornography and chat rooms during my preteen years. Once the free online software subscription ran out, we had to go to local libraries to use the computer. I recall when Yahoo had what they called "chat rooms."

Because of my "touching" experiences and additional curiosity, I found myself in conversations with presumably adult men in these chat rooms. They knew that I was a child but continued to chat and physically expose themselves to me anyway. I felt simultaneously admired by these men and confused. At the time, I wasn't aware of what pedophilia was and I was missing a father figure. These men were highly perverted predators. Now armed with the imagery from my chat room encounters, and having always been told I was a homosexual, I began to question my own sexuality. Thoughts crept into my mind. Maybe I was what they said I was. But this was against everything I believed. I began to question God. Lord, why have you allowed this? I struggled spiritually and otherwise. The peer rejection continued.

As I got older, I grew a bit taller, but also became a bit wider about my hips. These physical changes caused me great shame as I was already being teased for my mannerisms. I would always wear the baggiest clothes I could find and loosen my book bag straps low enough to cover my body. I began to hate myself. I hated the way I talked, the way I walked, the way I looked and everything else. I even hated to look in mirrors because I felt so ugly and unwanted.

By middle school, I had pretty much given up. All I thought about every day were ways to take my own life. I couldn't handle the rejection and humiliation anymore. I remember once coming home from school, sitting toward the back of the bus. Out of nowhere, I was struck in the back of my head. I had no clue who did it, but I started to cry. As we arrived at my stop, everyone laughed at me and threw things at me as I made my way to the front of the bus. I still get emotional thinking about that day. The kids lowered their windows to laugh at me some more as I crossed the street to my home. I threw my book bag across the street in anger. That was the day I begged my mother not to send me back to school.

My middle school was about eleven miles away from my home, and many days I would have to stand in the aisle of the school bus all the way to school as no one would let me sit with them. I remember on one occasion a young lady even bit me on my arm because I was determined to sit down somewhere on the bus and she had no one sitting with her. Because she was a female, rather than hit her, I started to pray. This was significant for me because usually, even though I was bullied, I never backed down from anyone even if I didn't think I could beat them. I would at least try to fight. Many of the school's professionals didn't know what I endured daily. They simply noticed that I always seemed to be in trouble, so naturally, they believed that I was always the troublemaker. Now don't get me wrong: Like the bullies, I also did things that I should not have. It wasn't until later in life that I realized that acting out was not the answer to rejection; a reality it took some time for me to embrace.

I continued to struggle with social interaction until I was finally kicked out of public school and sent to an alternative school, called Ogeechee Mental Health. Many of my teachers in public school felt that I must have had some mental or emotional issues to be in trouble continuously. I knew they felt this way about me, but I did not care. I didn't care about myself. I didn't care what happened to me.

I'll never forget the day my mother was called into my public school. The principal explained to her that they could no longer control my behavior and said that either I needed to be put on medication or be sent to an alternative school.

My mother refused medication but because I had so many problems and it stressed her so much, she accepted the recommendation of placing me in an alternative school. I would remain in alternative school from seventh to ninth grade.

I know it can be very difficult for educators to provide one-on-one attention to students when they have so many other students to consider. I would imagine that this has always been an issue within the public-school system. However, if we can't somehow connect with students on a personal level, it's likely that we will miss traits, attributes and characteristics that if otherwise fostered, could have set that young life on a road to personal success.

Interestingly enough and with a certain level of irony, as an adult I was asked to come back to my high school to share some words of encouragement with students in a behavior management class. By this point, I had become a successful registered nurse and father, a far cry from that alternative school little boy. I took great joy in this because, at one time, I was one of them. I had once sat in their seat.

The discussion went very well and warmed my heart to no end. I was honored and humbled at the same time. As I was leaving the school, I stopped by to bid farewell to one of the administrative staff that I remembered from my days in high school. This staff member had been a part of my county's school system for several decades and had had a role in educating practically everyone, or so it seemed. In speaking with her for the first time in many years, she stood there with a strange stare of admiration and confusion all rolled into one. It was a bit awkward and unsettling but nothing I hadn't experienced before.

After a few moments of superficial chatter, she asked, "Troy, when did you become this new person? I just don't remember you being so articulate and intelligent. What happened in your life that caused you to develop into 'this' new person? Maybe it can help us educators to identify these qualities to cultivate in our students earlier in their high school education, to push them in 'this' direction." I was taken aback by the question. I was confused as I didn't really understand what she was asking me. I didn't feel that I was any different overall than how I was when I attended high school under her leadership. I kind of smiled and rambled something to the effect of it being a good idea to provide diverse activities to support individual interests, a response that I hoped would end the conversation so that I could leave. It worked, and I did. I continued to smile as I left.

I didn't feel it was appropriate to share with that administrator my true feelings at that moment. I believe that only foolish people say everything they think all the time. But, I'll share my thoughts here. That staff member thought that I had changed in some drastic way, because after years of attending high school under her leadership, she never once got to know anything about me, so naturally, I appeared to be a different person altogether. She had written me off as that little boy that came to her school from an alternative school. To her, I was an afterthought, and my achieving any level of success was not likely. Statistically, in fact, that was relatively accurate.

For this reason, I don't feel that her attitude was intentional. I'm not sure and can't prove this, but I believe that after years in education, some educators develop biased views of certain types of students. This is in no way abnormal in my opinion. It's human nature. We all establish opinions based on personal experiences. However, I believe relying solely on our own experiences without remaining open-minded enough to know that one's own outlook is not the be-all and end-all in every situation, we severely stifle our ability to be effective.

I learned how easy it is to overlook things that are right in front of us...how we might prejudge someone based on who you think they are, not based on personal interactions with them, but on what you were told about them. Thus, we shut the door on people before having the opportunity to get to know them.

Chapter Thought: Your past doesn't have to dictate your future. That happens only if you let it. Make a choice today that no matter what conventional wisdom says, you are who God says you are and not necessarily your past! You can change. Who does He say you are now? You are the righteousness of God in Christ Jesus! You are more than a conqueror! You're the head and not the tail! You're an heir with Jesus, adopted into the first family of all first families! Are you excited about that? Me too!

CHAPTER THREE

"Iron sharpens iron, and one man sharpens another. "
Proverbs 27:17 (ESV)

~The Father I Never Had~

While in alternative school in the seventh through ninth grades, I faced a myriad of other challenges. They said I had a learning disability based solely on my behaviors (which is ironic because the disability was a supposed deficiency in reading and writing, but here I am writing my first book. Go figure!), and school officials tried to convince my mother I needed to be medicated. However, I did have some social issues, though not always my fault. For instance, one time I was sitting in my classroom waiting for the kitchen staff to bring lunch. A student came over to me and whispered, "When you get your food, give it to me." I thought this was some sort of dumb joke. Nowadays, it seems like something you'd see on a PBS special about bullying.

When my lunch arrived, the student came toward my desk to attempt to take my food. As I've mentioned before, I've never backed down as if afraid of anyone. This fellow was much larger than I, but there was no way I was going to let him take my lunch. As he reached for my food, I snatched it out of his hand and hit him in the face with the entire tray, and we began to fight. We were soon separated by teachers and staff, and I was escorted out of the class. I was placed in an empty wooden room that had no chairs, desk or anything but a dim fluorescent light in the ceiling. The room smelled of urine because other kids that had been placed there just urinated on the floor if there was no one to escort them to the bathroom. The staff took my belt and shoelaces, a practice that was said to reduce the likelihood of success of an attempted suicide. Here I was again, isolated in isolation.

However, all was not lost. While in alternative school, I met one of the greatest men I have ever known, which holds true even to this day. He was the principal, Dr. Hayward Cordy. Because of his broad shoulders and well above average height, he looked like a giant to me. He spoke with a deep rich voice that made everyone stop and take note. He had a presence that commanded respect, yet we could all see the compassion and love in his eyes for each of his students. I had never known anyone quite like that until that point.

I got into trouble many times while under his leadership. But each time I did, he treated me in a way that I had never experienced before by any teacher or leader. There were times where corporal punishment certainly was in order, back when it was still legal and encouraged. And he did not hesitate to mete it out. But each time he disciplined me, he did something that was completely foreign, to me. He'd hug me, and then say in his booming voice, towering over me, "Troy, I just want you to be better, I want you to do better, okay?"

Through my tears, I'd look up and say, "Yes sir." He'd hug me once more, then send me back to class. There were times I was taken out of class by Dr. Cordy himself and escorted to his office. Of course, I tried to figure out what I had done because surely, I was in trouble. I'd timidly walk in and take a seat. He'd continue to work at his desk saying very little, and even offer me some of his lunch without saying much. Then, after a while, he'd say, "You go on back to class now." It was in those small moments that I knew somebody cared about me, that somebody loved me even though I didn't always feel it. If no one else did, Dr. Hayward Cordy made me know that someone cared about me. With small, short, seemingly insignificant conversations, he always let me know he was concerned with what was happening in my life and that he was thinking of me. I had never had a male figure treat me with such genuine care. I admired him so much that I secretly wanted him to marry my mother, so he could become my real father. The father I never had. Still, to this day, I am forever grateful to have the opportunity to now think of him as "Dad," the father figure I so desired but never had.

Chapter Thought: Those of you that have opportunities to impact the lives of children, don't take that responsibility lightly. Children can be very difficult, but the love you invest in them now will, in the end, have been worth it. Even though you feel ineffectual at times, there may be someone watching you of whom you are totally unaware! Something that you think is small and insignificant, could be the very thing that helps someone to carry on, one more day. Continue to give of yourself even when you can't see the value in it. Somebody desperately needs what you have to offer!

CHAPTER FOUR

"And do not fear those who kill the body but cannot kill the soul. Rather fear him who can destroy both soul and body in hell." Matthew 10:28 (ESV).

~Searching for My Place in the World~

When I was about fifteen years old, my mother moved me, my sister and my little brother out to Houston, Texas, from Wadley, Georgia, so that my father could continue to attend a drug rehabilitation program he had enrolled in at a church called New Light, where Dr. I.V. Hilliard was the pastor. Texas was a whole new world for me. I attended Chester W. Nimitz Senior High School where I met some of the most exceptional people I had ever known up to that point in my life.

One of my closest friends (and 'brothers') to date, was named William, whom I met in our theater production at my new high school. I was cast alongside him in a play called, "One Flew Over the Cuckoo's Nest." I played the role of Dr. Spivey and my buddy William played one of the cuckoo characters in the insane asylum governed by the infamous Nurse Ratchet. William along with all my fellow cast members with their many eccentricities, made me feel free. I had never in my life felt so free, so free to be me. It was amazingly gratifying to be able to walk about in school and not be noticed by anyone. Not to stick out like a sore thumb. Not to continually look over my shoulder wondering who might be snickering, talking or pointing at me. Not to make purposeful detours to avoid certain groups of kids that might be lurking around a corner, sitting in a particular area. I could be invisible as I had always wanted to be. I began to fall in love with school and the many exciting opportunities it had to offer.

However, my home life was a struggle. My father, as I've said, was not nice to me. He was a menacing presence in and outside of the home. When he was around, an aura of anger, depression, gloom, sorrow and sadness all rolled into one filled every room of the house like a thick fog on a cloudy, dewy country morning. My siblings and I did all we could do to avoid him. Sometimes it worked; other times it didn't. After a short time in Houston, my mother discovered that my father was up to his old tricks again, womanizing and on drugs. My mother had uprooted our family and moved us all the way to Houston solely for my father's mental, spiritual and physical well-being. But he squandered her care and support again.

I love my father, but he's never been able to shake the oppressive influence of drugs. For my mother, this was the last straw. She had to move on. She had invested so much of her time, love, affection and attention into her marriage, but this was the end. So, one day my sister and I came home from school to find my mother there. She looked heavy and had very few words to say other than, "Your father is gone, and he will not be coming back." My sister and I started to jump up and down and shout, "Yes! Yes! Yes!" We were happy, so happy that he was gone.

But my mother stood there relatively expressionless. She looked at both of us and said, "Don't do that," and went off into her room and closed the door. I'm sure she shed many tears. She had lost the man she had loved since she was a teenager. Her husband was gone again, presumably for good. This had been the second time that my mother had married my father in an attempt to put her family back together. But here she was, alone again, a single mother of three. Earlier that day, my mother had put my father on a Greyhound bus and sent him back to New York, back to his mother, back to my birth place, back to where she first fell in love with him, Queens, New York.

While I loved Houston and the many relationships I had formed since being there, and was elated that dad was gone, there was one thing I did greatly miss about Georgia. Before leaving Georgia for Houston, Texas, a much older musician and church friend, "Eugene," and I had developed a singing group. The group was called Divine Connection but was later renamed J4-Twenty3. We had started on a few projects while trying to branch out and possibly do some touring in an attempt to try and land a record deal. But when my family moved to Texas, it put a big hitch in the groups plans.

Even though I was very happy living in Houston, I never forgot what we had started back in Georgia. I couldn't help but wonder what would've happened with the singing group had I not moved away. This idea chipped away at me until finally, when I was sixteen, I asked my mom if I could return to Georgia so that Eugene and I could continue our music endeavor. I wanted to pursue a career as a gospel artist. Eugene offered to allow me to live with him and his wife and reassured my mother that he would take care of me. Reluctantly my mother agreed. She later explained that she was not sure how things would turn out for me if I returned to Wadley, but she never wanted to be a parent who stood in the way of her children's dreams or goals. I also made the argument that I wanted to graduate with some people I grew up with. High school had become a lot better for me, much better than middle school. I didn't encounter the same bullying problems and was no longer picked on as I had been in elementary and middle school. I was comfortable with returning to Wadley and pursuing gospel music.

However, when I moved back to Georgia and in with Eugene, things didn't turn out exactly like I thought they would. I learned that some things work better in theory than in actual practice. Being only sixteen, I had minimal experience and knowledge, and was not yet a good judge of character. I didn't know that often times people may not want you as much as they want what you have to offer.

Now don't get me wrong, things went well in the beginning. However, I found that you truly get to know someone only after living with them. From the outside, everything was terrific. It looked as though we all lived in harmony. But behind closed doors, it was a very different story. Frequent physical fights became common. Here I was

at age sixteen having to fight again. Many nights I cried,
thinking I should return to Texas where I knew my mother
loved me. While lying on a tear-soaked pillow, I wondered if
anyone would ever truly love and want just me, not what I
could do, but just me, Troy.

In those moments I longed for my father to protect me,
to reassure me that I was loved, that I was enough, and that
everything would be okay. I was so far away from my mother
and had no father. It seemed that every male figure in my life
eventually rejected me for one reason or another.

At age seventeen, while still living in Georgia and
singing with Eugene, I finally got up the nerve to pursue a
girlfriend. At this point, I had only had one girlfriend in all my
life. Because of all of my teenaged insecurities, I didn't think
any girls in my high school ever really noticed me, much less
wanted to date me. I really liked the younger sister, of a friend
of mine. Her name was Pamela. I expressed my interest in her,
but like most other young ladies, she was not interested in me,
so I moved on. A few months later, through the juvenile high

school chatter, I learned that she might be a little attracted to me. One day, to be funny, I gave my cousin a note to give her. It was the old traditional letter that we all wrote in elementary school, merely saying, "Do you like me? Check YES or NO," and it had two checkboxes. She thought it was hilarious and decided to check YES. However, I later found out that Eugene, my roommate, didn't really like to see me happy. He attempted to convince Pam to treat me like other gals had, and even asked her why she would date someone like me. Thankfully, his attempts to turn her against me didn't work. From then on, Pam and I were inseparable.

Chapter Thought: Some situations don't work out the way they are planned, but that doesn't mean a dream dies there. Yes, there will be many people you encounter who will in one breath sing your praises, then in the next, yell, "Crucify him! Crucify him!" I'm here to tell you that that's okay! Yes! God has a plan for that, too! Remember, if it never rained, we wouldn't be able to appreciate the beauty of flowers, grass, trees and all living things. Storms can be uncomfortable but necessary to the continuation of life. Just put your head down and keep walking forward. Brush the rain from your eyes and take a deep breath. Eventually the storm will end, and you'll be glad it came and went!

CHAPTER FIVE

"Fear not, for I am with you; be not dismayed, for I am your God; I will strengthen you, I will help you, I will uphold you with my righteous right hand."
Isaiah 41:10 (ESV)

~The Great Escape~

Growing up as a young boy in the South, I always felt that even though I lived there, the rural South was not my home. I always longed to be in a larger city, in a more prominent place, around more people. I always felt that if I were in a larger town, I would be more accepted. While still in high school, as I've mentioned previously, I returned to Georgia from Texas to continue pursuing a singing career with a group I helped form call J4 Twenty3. This group became very popular in my small county and city. As the group's reputation grew, I became increasingly accepted by my peers at which time I met and started to date a young lady by the name of Pamela.

I found Pam to be beautiful, sweet, warm and kind. Because I had struggled so frequently with self-esteem issues, I couldn't believe that someone who looked like her and was as well liked as she was, would be interested in anyone like me. This new relationship produced feelings I had never experienced before. Feelings I wasn't sure what to do with. I grew up in a Christian home and being a young musician meant that I was always in church. The black church and its religious dogma was all I had ever known. By the time I was nineteen I was a licensed minister in my church. Because of my religious beliefs, I knew that Pam and I could not live a life that we considered sinful. So, although I was quite young, I asked Pam to marry me, and she agreed! We were just nineteen and eighteen when we tied the knot.

When I was twenty, I wanted us to move to a new city for a new start to accompany our new marriage. Nashville, Tennessee was my first choice, and Pam really had no preference and was fine with pretty much anywhere I wanted to go. As a musician, Nashville sounded to me like Disney World! During this preliminary period, I had spent a very short time singing background vocals for a fairly well-known gospel artist who told me that people who performed as we did, should live in Nashville, because it was a great place to learn about the music industry. He explained that I would get much needed experience and exposure to things in the industry I was not yet privy to.

Being young and very anxious to learn, I was convinced. At that time, I was working as a corrections officer in Georgia, but I knew that God had something else in store for me. I was ready to pursue new things, and Bartow, Georgia just wasn't the place for me anymore. Pam simply said, "Okay, let's do it."

So, over the next month, we sold most everything we owned. I needed all the money I could get to make the move happen. I was very young but had little fear of this transition. I figured, what have I got to lose? After all of our things were sold, my best friend Earl and I drove back and forth to Nashville looking at apartments, rental homes and anything else I could find within a certain price range, even if it would be just temporary housing.

I soon found an apartment complex that was willing to rent me a unit. Of course, I had no job. Being young and naïve I didn't care about that and figured it would all work itself out. We packed up the few things we still owned into one small U-Haul truck and hitched our tin-can-grey Chevy Lumina to the back of it, and we were off to Nashville, Tennessee, never to live in Bartow, Georgia again. I truly had no idea what lay ahead.

When we arrived in Nashville, with deposit money in hand, we went straight to the apartment complex that I had selected, and in the leasing office, sat down with the agent. We spoke briefly while she pecked some things into her computer. After a bit, she looked up at me and said, "Oh I'm sorry, but this will cost more than we told you." I was utterly taken aback by this because I had no extra money. Speechless, I looked across the table at the leasing agent as she looked back at me. My best friend Earl was with us at the time, and he too was flabbergasted. We looked at each other knowing neither of us had any more money.

Earl and I discussed it and decided that we would look for another apartment that day. We took Pam, her sister, and Earl's then fiancée to a mall parking lot to park the U-Haul with the Chevy attached. We asked them to stay there while we went to look for another place. Just a short way down the road we spotted another apartment complex that seemed promising. The leasing agent was very friendly and showed me an available unit that looked fine, and I told her I'd take it! She asked me to get some money orders to pay the fees and said Pam and I could move in that same day. I was overjoyed! I had about three hundred dollars in cash, just enough for the money orders we needed. Earl and I found a gas station that sold money orders, and I went in to buy them.

Then we returned to the leasing office to complete the paperwork. Again, the leasing agent seemed warm and welcoming, yet her demeanor had changed some. She went into a back office, and when she came out, it was like déjà vu. She said, "I'm sorry, but I can't rent you the apartment." My heart sank. She explained that the system would not allow her to process my application unless she could verify my employment. I wished she had told me that before I used the last bit of money I had to buy money orders! So, the decision was made for me. We could not stay in Nashville that night.

Earl and I went back to the mall to pick up the ladies, and we all drove back to Atlanta. I was devastated. In Atlanta, we got wind of an abandoned apartment that was unlocked, which we could use to sleep for the night. I planned to return to Nashville alone the next day, and all in one week, find myself a job, make some money, and get an apartment so that I could move Pam and her sister to Nashville. Crazy right?

How was I to accomplish this? I didn't know, but I believed that I could somehow do it.

I tried to sleep that night but couldn't. When I got up the next morning, I felt in my heart that I should take Pam and her sister back to Nashville with me. Earl and his then fiancé would not be returning with us. I didn't know how things would work out, but I believed they would. We got up and got dressed and got into the U-Haul with my Chevy Lumina still attached to the back. I started the U-Haul and sat for a moment. All I could do was pray because I had absolutely no plan.

I said, "Father, you know I have nothing in Nashville. We have no one there waiting for us and no home to go to. But Father, I have nothing here in Georgia either. I've sold all my possessions, and there's nothing for me to return to. So, Lord, as the children of Israel were led out of Egypt from under the tyranny of the Pharaoh, I believe you can provide a way of escape for us. The children of Israel had the Pharaoh's army behind them and the Red Sea in front of them. They had nowhere to go unless you parted the Red Sea. Father, I cannot go back. It's like Pharaoh's army is behind me and Nashville has a Red Sea in front of it. We need your grace and mercy to open up this Red Sea, so we can walk across into Nashville on dry land. In Jesus' name, Amen."

I put the truck into gear and we drove all the way back to Nashville. I knew very little about Nashville and found myself in an area called Cool Springs, Tennessee. I drove around this little city for a short time and noticed there were a few shops in the shopping complex that had 'Help Wanted' signs in the windows. One was a bookstore. I parked the U-Haul and went in. I told the manager that I knew I didn't look the part, and I knew I was not dressed to be interviewed, but I promised that if he gave me an application and allowed me the opportunity to work, he wouldn't be disappointed. The manager and I spoke for a little while longer, and before I knew it, the manager offered me the job.

When I returned to Pam and her sister who had waited in the U-Haul, I told them my great news! I had applied and had been hired on the spot. We drove for a bit more around the shopping complex, and I saw another Help Wanted sign in the window of a restaurant named Guido's New York Style Pizza Gourmet. I walked in and saw the place was beautiful. I saw other servers there, and I asked to speak with the manager. He came from the back and said they were looking for part-time servers and he would interview me. God, yet again, blew my mind. I was hired immediately. God was up to something! The Red Sea was parting before my eyes!

That evening, Pamela, her sister and I checked into an extended stay hotel. I had just enough money to pay for one week, but I still had another obstacle to clear. Since I never got the apartment I had intended to rent, I wasn't able to remove our things from the U-Haul, and the U-Haul's return date was fast approaching. While driving the next day, I noticed an advertisement for a storage unit with the "first month rent free." My U-Haul had to be returned the next day, and I knew we didn't need more than one month's storage. Problem solved!

My sister-in-law and I moved all of our stuff from the U-Haul into the storage unit, then drove the U-Haul back to a drop-off location, unhitched my Chevy Lumina, and headed back to the extended stay hotel. The next morning, I went to work at the bookstore and in the evening, I worked at the restaurant. During that first night, I made more money in tips than any of the other servers. No one seemed to believe that I had made that much money on my first night, so I had to show them. Again, God was up to something.

To save money, I ate leftovers at the restaurant each night so that the food we had at the hotel could be reserved for Pamela who was pregnant at the time. I worked for an entire week at both places and made enough money to start looking for a regular place to live again. This became a bit tricky because most of the money I made from the restaurant and bookstore would be needed to pay for another week at the hotel or we would have to move out, a potential vicious cycle.

Still, I searched and searched for a place for us to live. Every day that I could, I went to the library, and I looked in newspapers and checked the internet for some sort of apartment move-in special so that I could get me, my pregnant wife and her sister out of that extended stay hotel. After about three or four days I was down to the wire. I had to find somewhere to live fast, or I'd have to pay another two hundred and fifty dollars to renew the hotel lease, which would put me back in the same position I was in at the beginning of the week.

One day, I saw a tiny newspaper ad that read, "$99 Move-in Special." I was elated! I immediately jumped into my silver Chevy Lumina and drove over to Hermitage, Tennessee, a city in the Nashville metro area. I went in, met the leasing agent, and learned the process for leasing a unit. I had my ninety-nine dollars and was ready! She told me to purchase a money order for the application fee, and said that we would have to have the lights, water and all the utilities turned on before we could move in. This was all new to us novices, as none of us had rented anything before.

By this point, we were down to our last day. I had moved us out of the extended stay hotel to save money. I needed every dime I could save to get the utilities turned on and not pay for another week at the hotel. During this week I had spoken with a pastor friend of mine and shared with him how we were doing. He was so gracious, and out of the goodness of his heart, he sent fifty dollars to help us. It went towards a different hotel room for the night we left the extended stay place.

I was scheduled to meet the leasing agent the next day to get moved in, so the next morning we woke up very early to get our things together and check out. We all jumped in the car and drove around Nashville to pay for all the utilities to be turned on, which took almost the entire day. By the time we drove back to Hermitage, the leasing office was closing. We had no place to go. I had already checked us out of the hotel room.

As I pulled up to the leasing office, the agent was locking the door behind her. She had clocked out for the day, but when she saw my pregnant wife and I pull up in our Chevy, she graciously unlocked the office door and let us in.

God is always on time. We finished up the paperwork and showed her that all the utilities were in my name. She took us down to the duplex apartment we had just leased, handed me the keys, and said, "Congratulations!"

I unlocked the door, and we all went into 432 Tyler Drive, our new home. We were officially citizens of Nashville, Tennessee. All three of us sat down on the floor of that empty apartment with tears in our eyes. All we could say was, "Thank you, Lord, for your grace, mercy and favor!" He had opened the sea for us! This all transpired over one week and boy what a week!

Chapter Thought: Anything worth having is worth fighting for. If God gives you a dream, go after it with all of your heart; with fervor! He'll be with you! I once heard the legendary gospel singer Shirley Caesar say, "If God cracked the door, I'd kick it down!" One of my heart's desires is to leave this world completely drained. I want to be emptied of everything that God put in me to give to the world. I don't want to take anything with me! Do you feel the same? If you do, you can't accomplish it by allowing the fear of the unknown to dictate how you move through this world. Step out on faith! God honors faith! It pleases Him to see you take steps based on faith! Go for it, my friend! God's got you covered! "Trust in the Lord with all your heart, and do not lean on your own understanding. In all your ways acknowledge him, and he will make straight your paths." Proverbs 3:5-6 (ESV)

CHAPTER SIX

*"I repeat, be strong and brave! Don't be afraid and
don't panic, for I, the Lord your God, am with you in
all you do." Joshua 1:9 (NET)*

~Adventures of a Determined Father~

A lthough I never really knew much about manhood, one thing I did know was that I always wanted to be a father. When I was a young boy, I longed to have that father-son relationship with my dad. Whether you are male or female, a mother, son, daughter or uncle, the role of a father is one that is unmatched. My hat goes off to all the courageous single mothers out there. Without you, none of us would be here. We salute you daily for your sacrifices!

But the void that an absentee father leaves in the life of his son is one that a young man can spend a lifetime trying to fill. For me, that void was filled in ways I later realized, were in fact, self-destructive. I learned that these pitfalls only made life worse and heaped on more and more layers of trouble that I would have to one day strip away to be free. One of my greatest fears was that I wouldn't be a satisfactory father to my own children and that they would battle with the same demons I had struggled with all my life.

One of the greatest moments in my life happened also to be one of the scariest. It was when my first son, Troy Jr., was born. I was only twenty-one years old, and Pam was just twenty. We found ourselves in a relatively empty hospital in Dalton, Georgia. All I remember about the hospital is how mute and neutral all the colors were and how empty it seemed. Pam and I were completely alone. No family or friends or loved ones. Just us preparing for our first-born son to draw his first breath. I'll never forget the moment he was born. One thing that was different about my oldest son from the rest of my children is that, even in the womb, he was very stubborn. He kept flipping over and turning into the wrong position for delivery. We knew then that he would be a strong-willed young man much like his father! When I saw my son enter this world it was surreal; seeing this new life that had been created from Pam and me.

Many questions, thoughts and ideas ran through my head as I cut the umbilical cord and listened to my baby cry. I felt a love for him I had never felt for another living thing. I would give my life for him without question. I had always wondered what kind of father I would be having never been fathered myself. What did I know about this role? Nothing! I would often jokingly tell people that if I didn't know anything else about fatherhood, I knew what it was not.

I was, however, certain of a few things. I knew I would never leave my children or forsake them under any circumstances. I was certain that I would never knowingly cause them to feel unsupported, and I would always do everything I could to show them unconditional love no matter who they became or what they did. I would work my fingers to the bone to provide for them, and I would show them my best example of a good man and a father, one they could always depend on for protection. One who's love for them outweighed any of his own personal struggles.

The reality is that all these things have been very difficult for me to enact because I did not have them consistently in my own life. It was much like promising to give a stellar performance in a play without having even read the script. I had an idea of the role I should play, but what are my lines? There was no text of which to refer. Of all the items I listed above, only one came naturally to me…working, which I've been doing since I was eleven.

As I mentioned earlier, my very first job, at age eleven, was in an auto parts store owned by an older fellow named Billy Weeks. After that, I was never without a job for long periods of time. From jobs in factories to jobs in fast food, I believed in working. I remember being in nursing school, while working 50 plus hours a week in food service. I either went to work, to school or both seven days a week for an entire year. You see, I not only took pride in the work that I did, but also in making good on the promise to always do whatever it took to provide for my children. I remember when my grandfather found out that I was getting married at the tender age of nineteen, the only thing he said to me was, "Troy, just take care of your family." His admonition, "Troy, just take care of your family," has reverberated in my head ever since. Indeed, it's what I do.

God never promised that every moment would be easy for us, especially as parents. While I took great pride in being a good provider, even the strongest among us has to face the reality that our human bodies are finite. I recall one morning in particular, after the birth of my second son, Trevor, I awoke with a searing, burning pain in my stomach. At the time I was working at the Nashville international airport as a retail supervisor and had to be at work at 4:15 AM. Can you believe that? Whew, that's early! But I digress. I would get up at about

three most days, but on this day, I woke up before my alarm
clock went off and I just couldn't go back to sleep.

This pain in my stomach was becoming increasingly
uncomfortable. It grew closer to the time that I would have
normally been on my way to work, so I decided to call in and
let them know that I could not make it due to the pain in my
stomach. I rolled over, and I told Pam I was going to stay
home from work. Anyone that knows me knows that I do not
like to miss work. I don't know why, but I feel like I am wasting
my day if I don't go to work, even if I really need to stay home.
Maybe it's because all I've ever done is work and view it as a
part of my fatherly duties.

Later in the morning, I got up and went to Wal-Mart
to buy some over-the-counter medications to soothe my upset
stomach. However, the pain got worse as the day went along.
It got so bad while I was driving that I had to pull over.
Thankfully, I was near an emergency room, so I walked in. At
that time, I did not have any medical insurance. I couldn't
afford it (this was prior to Obamacare!), so naturally, they did

not want to treat me. They ran no tests and did no radiology, but just gave me some over-the-counter medication and told me to go home. They said that if my pain increased, I should go back to an ER. I imagine they wanted to say, "Not this ER but to another ER!" Bent over in pain by this point, I limped back to my car and slowly drove myself home.

When I arrived, all I could do was fall on the floor in the living room and curl up into a ball. My stomach hurt so badly that I could not stand. Pam, studying to be a medical assistant at the time, was headed out to class, but seeing me on the floor in the fetal position, she asked if I was okay. I said I would be fine (typical male response, right?). Up until this point, I'd never had any major health problems. Any health issues I did have had been very minor, so I figured like all other issues, this too would pass. But Pam didn't feel comfortable leaving me there like that. After all, we then had two infant children that needed care. She finally convinced me that we needed to go back to the ER.

It's How You Finish

I got into the passenger seat, and she drove. By this point, I was in tears. My insides felt like I had ingested molten lava! We got to the ER, and I finally saw the physician. I was lying on the examination table and an older white-haired doctor walked in. He looked at me briefly and then out of nowhere, he struck the bottom of my right foot with his fist. This is an old school technique used to checking for appendicitis. I almost screamed! He then proceeded calmly to tell me that my appendix was about to rupture. He explained that I needed to be admitted so that he could do surgery on me the next morning. I agreed to it all the while thinking I could not stay in the hospital for a long time. I had to return to work, thinking that if I didn't work, we didn't eat. For me, that was not an option.

After a day post-surgery, I was discharged from the hospital, and the day after returning home, I went back to work. With holes in my stomach from the surgery, I limped around, bracing my stomach with one hand and keeping my balance with the other. Each step was torture. As the day went along, that familiar but unusual pain returned. Again, it got progressively worse, so I left work and had to return to the ER where I was told I had a massive stomach infection from the surgery and had to be readmitted to the hospital. After a few days in the hospital on IV antibiotics, I was better and able to go home, this time, to stay.

I share these stories not to boast of bravery or to prove how strong a man or father I am. Rather, I want to convey how seriously I took my grandfather's words, "Troy, just take care of your family." I believe that all real fathers will move heaven and earth to care for their babies.

It's funny how telling one story seems to remind you of another. I had been having some major car trouble. The Chevy Lumina was out of our lives and the only car I had broken down during a trip back to Georgia. I managed to get my family back to Nashville due, yet again, to my brother Earl and his lovely now wife coming to the rescue. However, once back in Nashville, I had a new dilemma. I had no car. I called my mom and I asked if she would send me fifty dollars so that

I could buy a bicycle for transportation to work. She sent the money and I bought the bike. I joked with Earl the day before I returned to work that it would be "funny" if it rained the next day.

When I woke up at three AM and got myself ready to head to work on my bike, there it was: torrential rains. Pam awoke with me, looked outside and said, "You just need to stay home today." Again, I repeated my faithful saying, "If I don't work, we don't eat." I wrapped my shirt in a plastic bag, put on the biggest hooded coat I had, jumped on that bicycle and took off down the road in the rain.

To get to the main access road from my apartment, I had to ride the bike up a relatively steep incline. About halfway up the slope, the chain on the bike broke. All I could say to myself was, My Lord; please tell me this is not happening. At that point, I knew I couldn't ride any longer, so I took off, running the bike back to my apartment to put it inside, and then ran down the street. I was going to be late for work if I didn't hurry. I figured if I couldn't ride the bike to work, I would have to run there in the rain.

The rain wasn't so bad but what made this situation the most uncomfortable was seeing many of my co-workers whizzing by in their cars as I alternated between walking and running. By the grace of God and some fancy footwork, I made it to work on time, albeit soaked from the waist down. What won't a father do to provide for his babies?

A few days later while walking home from work, I decided to take pictures of my feet and of the street behind me. Even in that dark season, I chose to meditate on victory. I can't find those photos now, but I took them because I wanted to remember that moment vividly because I knew I would not be in it forever. I knew there was something greater awaiting me. Moments like these helped me understand and appreciate the blessings of God. Andraé Crouch wrote in a song, "For if I'd never had a problem, I'd never know that God could solve them, I'd never know what faith in The Word of God could do."

It's How You Finish

While I've always prided myself on being a good provider, the very thing that I took so much satisfaction in, began to take a toll on me and my relationships as time went along. My marriage began to suffer due to the constant stress and strain on me both in and outside the home. Having four children meant that Pam was pregnant during many of our early years. That left me to carry the load of financial responsibility and left me feeling quite alone.

Each of Pam's pregnancies was physically very stressful for her. Each time she was pregnant, she had to leave her job because she didn't feel well enough to work, and even at home, she couldn't cook because the smells made her nauseous. She couldn't clean because she was too tired, and she couldn't even do the laundry as it was too physically taxing. I tried to be as understanding as I could, but it proved to be too much for me.

I knew she wasn't behaving this way on purpose, but deep down I began to resent her. I felt that I was carrying far more than my share of the family burden. Each day I left our home before the children woke up, to go to class, as I was in school at this time. Then from school, I'd head straight to work to close the fast food restaurant at midnight. I was very tired and felt I had no help at all. Leaving before my children woke up and not getting back home until they were already back in the bed was rough. Whenever I did have off time, I cleaned the house, washed clothes, and cooked. Pam was unable to help me during these times. But the issue of household chores was definitely not the only problem we had. In fact, it wasn't even the major concern. Insecurities played the biggest role in the breakdown of our marriage, which I'll discuss in more detail in the next chapter.

As my sons got a little older, I started to see many of the same traits and characteristics that I displayed when I was their age. To be honest, this frightened me. I never wanted my sons or any of my children, including my daughter, to experience the hurts, fears and insecurities that I did. The thought of this moved me to tears. To think that my children would ever have to experience the mental and emotional battles of their father was too much for me to handle.

It's How You Finish

One day, I received some minor disappointing news about one of my sons from his teacher. True enough, children misbehave, but for some reason, it rocked me to my core, so much so that I called him to the living room along with my other sons. Tearfully, I started to pray for my three sons from the depths of my heart and plead with God not to allow my sons to experience the things their father did. I prayed that God protect them from battles with self-esteem, sexuality, love and rejection that their father still battled with to that day. I guess in my heart and mind, I felt that I had barely held on through all of those struggles, which made me question whether my children would be able to endure the same concerns. I'm pretty sure that when I began to pray for my sons, they must've thought their father was losing it. As I prayed and laid hands on them, I cried out to God to break all generational curses from them, to break all spirits of lust, perversion, and lasciviousness, and to bind all spirits of hatred and anger, bitterness and jealousy. I cried out that they would live healthy, successful, normal lives, and have the childhood that I never had. I beseeched God that I could be to them what my father never was to me.

Chapter Thought: You don't have to know "the way," to know there is one. I had no concept of what it truly meant to be a father, but I knew that there was a way for me to do it anyway. In one of Paul's letters to the church in Philippi, he explains that through Christ, he was able to achieve victory in any situation! He wrote, "I know what it is to be in need, and I know what it is to have plenty. I have learned the secret of being content in any and every situation, whether well fed or hungry, whether living in plenty or in want. I can do all this through him who gives me strength." Philippians 4:12-13 (NIV).

You have everything you need to make it through whatever situation life and living throws at you! God promised that where we are weak, He is strong. It's not easy to do, but we must cast all of our cares on God because He cares for us! Have peace in knowing that you don't have to have all the answers as long as you know the one who does! And after

you've done all you can to keep standing, stand some more!

CHAPTER SEVEN

"...for you know that the testing of your faith produces steadfastness. And let steadfastness have its full effect, that you may be perfect and complete, lacking in nothing." James 1:3-4 (ESV)

~A True Test of My Faith~

While living in Tennessee I took on a job working for a Krystal restaurant as the assistant general manager. One night fairly late, while headed home from work, I was stopped by a police officer just as I was turning into the entrance of my apartment complex. I knew that I wasn't speeding, and my license plate wasn't expired either, so I was unsure why I was being stopped. I pulled into a parking space in front of my apartment building and turned off the motor as the officer approached my car door. He hit my window with his hand, I suppose to get my attention, while shining his flashlight in my eyes.

I opened my car door to ask the officer why he was stopping me. I was exhausted and ready to go to bed. To my surprise, the officer slammed my door shut and yelled for me to roll down the window. Since the motor was off, I was unable to get the window down. Being that I was at my home, I opened the door and stood up to ask the officer what this was all about. I didn't think much of the situation as I didn't consider myself to be a threat in any way. I assumed the officer would see that I was a professional, as I was wearing a white shirt, necktie, and casual pants. It's hard to believe that I looked intimidating or threatening to anyone, but I suppose he became afraid.

The officer immediately attacked me. He struck me in the face, breaking my plastic-framed glasses right down the center so that I could no longer see anything! It was about 1 o'clock in the morning, so it was very dark out. He began to try to pull me down to the ground, saying, "Get on the ground, get on the ground!" All the while, I was asking why he was doing this, and what I had done wrong. Obviously, before he had even stopped me, he had called another officer for backup, because shortly after he started trying to wrestle me to the ground, another officer came out of nowhere and jumped on my back.

In the midst of the struggle, I fell to the ground, and both officers got on top of me. The original officer screamed at me to stop resisting and to put my hands behind my back. Being that my glasses broke when the initial officer hit me in the face, I was terrified. As I lay on the ground, one officer put his knee on my head and the other put his knee on my back, and they struck and punched me in my side. Then they started saying something I couldn't believe I was hearing. They started calling me Nigger. I felt like I was dreaming.

You see and hear of things like this on TV and in movies, but you never think that anything like this would ever happen to you. The Trayvon Martin case in Florida was still a media sensation at this time, however, I felt the spirit of the Lord come over me. The only thing I could say each time they hit me was that I loved them. It might sound strange, but thats all that would come out in that moment. Following each of their punches I said, "I love you anyway." It was truly a God moment for me. As the officers continue to scream, "Put your hands behind your back and stop resisting," I tried to explain that one of my arms was under my body and with them sitting on top of my body, I could not get my arm out. I expressed that I was in no way resisting. The other officer, who had my other arm, was bending it against the joint. If he continued to bend it that way, it felt like he was going to break it. Again, in spite of his actions and the possibility of a badly broken arm, all I could say was that I loved them anyway, and that even if he broke my arm, I'd still love him.

I could tell that the officers started to feel a bit strange about what was going on because they quieted down somewhat and stopped talking to me. I felt helpless and alone.

All I could do was pray, which may have freaked the officers out even more because I wasn't praying in English. I started praying in my heavenly language, also known as "tongues," (see Acts Chapter 2 of the King James version of the Holy Bible) because nothing else would come out. By this time, several other officers had arrived. My apartment complex parking lot was filled with a sea of blue flashing lights and police everywhere. Some of my neighbors came out onto their balconies to see what was going on. I should mention that I don't actually remember saying some of the things to the police I've shared here. Strange right? Later, bystanders would share with me some of the things they heard me saying. But, by the grace of God, two young ladies were standing at their window when the officer initially stopped me and witnessed the physical altercation between the police and me.

After I was handcuffed, picked up off the ground, and put in the back seat of a police car, I still had no idea what I had done or why I had even encountered these police officers. One of the officers who had arrived later came over to speak with me. He asked what I thought were unusual questions, including if I was a student at Tennessee State University in the nursing program. I tried to see who he was because it seemed he already knew me. However, I could not make out his face because of the tears in my eyes coupled with the darkness outside. Of course, I also didn't have my glasses that lay broken beneath my car in the parking lot.

As he continued questioning me, his voice became familiar, and I recognized the outline of his face. I knew him! This was one of my college classmates. He and I had spoken in class, about how he did not want to be a police officer anymore but wanted to try nursing. When I realized who it was, I told him that he knew me, and he knew that I wouldn't do anything that would jeopardize my life, education or career. But all he could say was that he had to act on what he'd been told by the other officers.

He went on to tell me that the initial officer had told the other officers that when he stopped me, and I opened my door, I stood up and attacked him! He said that I had pushed him backward, causing him to fall back and hit his head on a truck parked behind him. He told them that I was on top of him and I had completely overpowered him, and that he and his fellow officer had to use force to stop me from resisting.

When I heard what the officer told his colleagues I had done, I was completely dumbfounded. I could not believe that he had made up such an elaborate lie. The things he said I did, I would never do to anyone, let alone a police officer. A few of the officers came over to the car that I was in, leaned their heads in and used some choice words in reference to me, and made a few threats before slamming the door. I said nothing more. Again, all I could do was pray.

When I arrived downtown, I was taken to be booked, and my handcuffs were removed. During this process, the officer taking my fingerprints asked what had happened. She noticed how I was dressed and seemed to figure that the charges didn't match my appearance. She didn't share with me what I was charged with at that time but did provide the officers reason for stopping me: the tint on my windows was too dark, she said! Mind you I had purchased this car only a few months before, and the windows came tinted. I had no idea it was an issue. The officer then leaned in close to me and said, "You need to get a lawyer." After that, she stared briefly at me but said nothing more.

I was taken to a video call system in another relatively small room within the jail. I saw a small television screen and noticed an older Caucasian gentleman looking back at me. He motioned for me to pick up the telephone that was on the right-hand side of the screen. I complied and listened. He explained that I had been charged with assaulting a police officer and resisting arrest, and that my bond would be $30,000 total, $20,000 for the assault and $10,000 for resisting arrest.

At this point, I still had not said another word. I was completely flabbergasted and in shock. I thought I was dreaming! The gentleman on the screen asked me if I had any questions, to which I slowly and hesitantly muttered, "No sir." I still could not see anything clearly. I could see figures moving around me, but without my glasses, I could not see faces. They put me in a holding cell with about twenty other men. By this point, it was about three o'clock in the morning.

Before all this had occurred, I planned to go home, eat a bowl of Raisin Bran, shower and hit the sack because I was scheduled to be back at work the next morning. But, obviously, none of that happened. I found myself in jail in downtown Nashville, still completely confused as to why I had been stopped to begin with. I couldn't help but wonder what I had done to deserve this.

It's in times like this you find out who's really with you. Some are just with you in words but not in actions. The first person I could think to call was someone I knew was with me in both words and actions; my best friend Earl. I knew I could rely on him. It was the middle of the night, so naturally he and his now wife were asleep. I had to call several times before he answered and accept the charges from an inmate in the Davidson County Jail. What an introduction, right? With tears in my eyes and a trembling voice, I tried to calm myself enough to explain to my best friend Earl, of whom I refer to as my brother, what had just happened to me as much as I understood it.

The only thing my brother said was, "I'm gonna come to Nashville and get you out. I'll call your mom, but you will not be in jail another day." If you ever find a best friend like that, cherish them for a lifetime. I thanked my brother, then called and spoke with my mom. My brother found out my bail amount and without hesitation sent my mom the money needed for my bail so that I could get out of jail that day. No one has ever had my back as much as my best friend and brother, Earl. It's amazing when you have someone in your life who without a shadow of a doubt, will come running to help you if ever you need them, no questions asked. I'm forever grateful to Earl and thank God for him.

Later that morning, as I sat waiting along with several men who had been arrested the night before, my name was called. My bond had been posted, and I was free to go, but would have to return on my court date for a hearing.

However, I had been taken to the county jail, so I had no way home. The bail bondsman offered me a ride home, and when I arrived, I saw the interior of my car was a mess. I assumed the police had searched for drugs or weapons, but of course, they found nothing.

As I headed to work, two young women ran up to me in the parking lot of my apartment complex, to ask if I was okay. I didn't know who they were, but I told them I was fine, and I appreciated them asking and their concern. One of them said, "We saw everything! We saw those police officers attack you! We watched the whole thing from beginning to end! If you need us to come to court with you as witnesses, we will do it for you!" I became very emotional, as God had a ram in the bush for me, yet again.

Naturally, I didn't know how this court thing would play out for me as it would be my word against that of several white police officers. A few days later was my hearing before the unforgettable Judge Casey Moreland. By this time, my uncle had sent me some money for an attorney as we all felt that this was a case of police brutality, racial profiling, and discrimination. My attorney was upfront and honest as he explained that this would be a difficult case because I was a young, African-American male vehemently denying the claims of young, white police officers in Nashville, Tennessee, and it would more than likely not work out in my favor. In my opinion, African-American men in the US, are truly guilty until proven innocent.

On the day of the pre-trial hearing, the two women who had witnessed the whole event from their apartment window, showed up just as they had promised. My heart was overjoyed! I had given them the date and time of the pre-trial hearing. They were both there on time and ready to testify! I knew that they didn't have to do this for me. When the district attorney got wind of the fact that not one, but two witnesses showed up to testify on my behalf, she and the police officers started to scramble. I'm sure they assumed there were no witnesses in my case, but these two honorable, beautiful young women stood up for me. I am forever grateful and will never forget them. My rams in the bush!

My attorney asked me if I wanted to speak at the pre-trial hearing to attempt to persuade the judge to consider dismissing this case. He made it clear that this was not a common practice, but we could take the chance and see what would happen. I agreed to it because I had nothing to hide and greatly desired to explain my side of the story. However, this would turn out to be one of the most traumatic events I ever experienced.

After the hearing began, my attorney called me to the stand. The judge asked my attorney if he was sure he wanted to call me to the stand, as if the judge was certain nothing would change his mind about what he already thought he knew. My attorney assured him that I wanted to testify on my behalf and I understood the risk involved.

As I took my seat on the stand, the judge glanced over with a sinister look in his eyes and said, "Are you sure you want to do this?" I confirmed that I did, and he sat back and said, "Okay, go ahead."

The assistant district attorney started to question me about the whole incident, making many condescending remarks and saying things to challenge my intelligence, like had I ever seen cop movies. I maintained my composure even as my attorney repeatedly objected to much of what the assistant district attorney was asking. On the night of the incident, there were only two officers present during the initial altercation, but in the courtroom, sitting at the plaintiff's table, were five or six police officers ready to testify against me, including some who had not even witnessed what occurred.

As I told my story, several of the officers laughed or snickered at me, to be as disrespectful as possible. The judge said nothing. About halfway through my testimony, the judge became very angry at my attorney's objections. He yelled that he was angry at the thought of me "sitting up here lying." When Judge Moreland said that, I muttered in a whispered voice, "My goodness."

Judge Moreland overheard me and screamed, "What did you say?" I paused, stunned. I was so afraid and didn't know how to respond, so I told him that I had said, "Yes sir." I felt like a bleeding calf in a pool of piranha. I had no idea why the judge was so upset and angry with me when he didn't even know me. The look in his eyes was so cold and evil. I thought he wanted to kill me. My attorney then stated that perhaps the judge might be biased because of who I was in relation to the plaintiffs. This further infuriated Judge Moreland, and he screamed at both me and my attorney stating that he hoped my attorney was not insinuating that he, the judge, was making his decisions based on race. Judge Moreland said his decisions were based on the facts and that was why he was binding my case over to the grand jury. With a slam of the gavel, the hearing was over. He never even heard from my witnesses. Thankfully though, I never stood before judge Moreland again.

I returned to court multiple times over the next two years, during which time I couldn't get a job because background checks revealed the assault on a police officer and resisting arrest charges, even though they were both still pending. At one point I told my then wife I was tired of fighting and going back and forth to court. I wanted to plead no contest to get it all over with.

The day I headed to court intending to plead no contest, I remembered something my then wife Pam said, "If you did not do it, don't say that you did." I stood before the judge with about eleven other young men, all of us planning to plead either no contest or guilty before this new judge. The judge went down the line asking each one for his plea, and each man pled guilty or no contest. I was the third or so person from the end that the judge addressed. He asked, "How do you plead?" Reluctantly, I said, "No contest."

The judge accepted it and moved to the next fellow in line. After a few moments, he had all of our pleas. The judge began to explain how to complete the plea process. However, I was having trouble focusing on what he was saying because, in my heart, I felt that I had given up. I started to think about my sons, young black males. I began to consider whether I was providing the right example for them. Would I ever want them to cower away and plead no contest, taking whatever an [at times] unjust justice system decides to throw at them?

As the judge was still speaking, I interrupted, to say, "Judge, I'm sorry. I cannot do this. I did not do what I was accused of, and I cannot stand here and say that I did, or even plead no contest." I told the judge I wished to retract my plea and explained that I wanted to plead not guilty and go to trial. If nothing else, I wanted the chance to show my sons that you never cringe and allow injustice to prevail. You don't back down, but instead stand up for what is right, what is true and what is honorable. The other young men looked at me with wide eyes.

This being a new and more compassionate judge than Moreland, he looked at me and said, "Young man, are you sure?" Holding my head high, with thoughts of my sons flooding my mind, I said, "Yes sir, I'm sure." My attorney looked at me in total shock because he had no idea I was about to do what I had just done. He and I had a short conversation afterward and discussed with the assistant district attorney, dates for the next hearing. So, countless times over the next two years, I went to court, and each time I went, the assistant district attorney requested a new hearing date for various reasons. These two years would turn out to be some of the hardest of my life. My electricity was turned off during this period, and my only viable vehicle was repossessed.

To protect them, I sent my young family back to Georgia from Nashville. However, I refused to give up on what I had been working for so hard. With no car, food or electricity, I put my head down and barreled through to completion of my nursing degree. God blessed me with an angel who helped me get to school each day, a classmate with a heart of gold, and to boot, her name was Faith! To complete my homework assignments, I took my tiny laptop computer to McDonald's to use their Wi-Fi. My mom sent me a few dollars every now and then, and I bought a few double cheeseburgers and took a ton of napkins. Why all the napkins? Well if you can't afford to purchase tissue, then...well, I think you get the picture!

Any food I brought home I hung up on a nail in the wall in front of the mattress on which I slept. Why did I do this? Well, the apartment complex was overrun by roaches. Hanging a bag on the wall allowed me to see any roaches trying to get to my food. Previously, I had left my food on the floor near me one night and awoke to find it covered in roaches. Gross? Yes! But I share this to encourage you that God is a deliverer! How do I know? He did it for me! I've seen Him do it and I'm confident He'll do it for you! Let these stories increase your faith!

After those two grueling years filled with many more incidents, God saw fit to allow this storm to subside. After moving back to Georgia after the completion of my nursing degree at Tennessee State University, I returned to Nashville, Tennessee for what would be the final hearing, the one that normally would precede a trial, but God had other plans. Out of nowhere the district attorney spoke with my attorney and stated that they decided to drop all charges against me. I'm not sure but I assume it was because it would be too difficult to prove at trial that I had assaulted anyone or resisted arrest, with two witnesses refuting these claims. The district attorney never explained why the charges were dropped. I was simultaneously thrilled and in shock. Finally, I would get my life and clean record back! God had prevailed again!

But that's not the end of the story. You see, God has a way of "turning the tables," so to speak. His word tells us that vengeance is His: "Beloved, never avenge yourselves, but leave it to the wrath of God, for it is written: 'Vengeance is mine, I will repay, says the Lord.'" (Romans 12:19 ESV) Remember Judge Casey Moreland, the first judge I saw? A number of years later he was arrested and charged with bribery and embezzling money, for which he pled guilty. "Do not be deceived: God is not mocked, for whatever one sows, that will he also reap." (Galatians 6:7 ESV)

Chapter Thought: Because we live in this flesh, it's easy to believe the fight is against flesh and blood, but God teaches that this natural world pales in comparison to the activity in the spirit. When you have greatness in you, you should expect a spiritual war to be waged against you often! It simply means you are a tremendous threat to the kingdom of hell. But remember that God's word tells us, "The LORD will fight for you; you need only to be still." Exodus 14:14 (NIV) And we all should believe that "When the enemy shall come in like a flood, the Spirit of the Lord shall lift up a standard against him." Isaiah 59:19 (KJV)

CHAPTER EIGHT

"Forgetting what is behind and straining toward what is ahead,
I press on toward the goal to win the prize for which God has
called me heavenward in Christ Jesus. "
Philippians 3:13-14 (NIV)

~I Said, "I Do," Then Didn't~

Marrying as teenagers presents its own set of challenges no matter who you are. You don't even really know yourself yet. It can be very difficult to intertwine two lives before they are fully established in their own right. For me, as an insecure, introverted young man, marriage proved to be a challenge for which I was not yet ready. My timidity and apprehensiveness ran so deep that for the first year of my eleven-year marriage I refused even to take my shirt off in front of my wife. I thought that I was so unappealing, unattractive and undesirable that no one would want to see me that way.

I had a bit of what's called body dysmorphic disorder or BDD. What I saw in the mirror didn't match reality but was a warped perception of my own reflection. Being married to an insecure man is dangerous for many reasons. Many self-doubting men treat the people they're in a relationship with out of the reservoir of their feelings about themselves. If an insecure man hits his wife or partner, he's hitting himself. If he speaks down, he's projecting how he feels about himself. If he treats his partner with disdain without cause, he very much dislikes himself. While I was never physically abusive to my wife, I was unable to give her the love and caring treatment she deserved because I did not love or care for myself.

Insecurities are closely tied to and intertwined with feelings and emotions related to rejection and can cause one to do things that they know are abnormal. When we feel rejected, or insecure, we may project that on others by rejecting them. And whatever it is we feel insecure about, causes us to build an expectation of further rejection from those around us, even if those feelings are unfounded.

We all have a fundamental need to belong and are sometimes willing to "wear a mask" if we feel that that's what is needed to belong. So, we wear the facade we've grown to believe people around us consider socially acceptable irrespective of what we actually "look like." We all just want to be loved. From the time we can interact socially, we all want to be accepted by someone or some group or something. When we are deprived of that as a child, we can grow into adults who walk around with extreme fear of rejection. Consciously or not, we recall how painful it was when were children, and through our own evolution we develop skills, traits and abilities to hide in plain sight to avoid experiencing the turmoil and heart-wrenching pain of our childhood rejections.

Rejection played a very critical role in my life. As a child rejected by both peers and adults, I learned how to put up a front. Thus, as an adult, people often told me, "Troy, it seems like nothing anyone says or does ever bothers you." But that wasn't true at all. Once, someone said something negative about my appearance, and then added, "Nothing people say bothers Troy. He doesn't care what anyone else thinks." But what they didn't know is how that small, seemingly insignificant critique about my appearance, shattered me and ruined the rest of my day. I focused on that one thing; playing it over and over in my mind. To others, this may have been something very insignificant, and to this day I don't remember what was said, but I do remember how it made me feel.

As I grew older, I somehow became more appealing to other adults. People complimented me, and I'd look at them in a state of confusion. They'd say things like, "Troy, you look nice," or "You're so handsome," and I'd look back completely bewildered and say, "Really?" As an adult, I honestly could not believe that someone found me attractive after so many years of rejection. This was a revelation to me, a brand-new space for me, and I liked it. In fact, I liked it to a fault. I started to chase those compliments and feelings of acceptance. I wanted this new feeling to continue. In moments of vulnerability, it did not matter if the attention came from males or females. I just wanted to be accepted, loved and admired, something I'd never had.

This desire for acceptance took me down a road filled with lust and sexual trysts I'd never thought I'd experience. In order not to be too graphic in this book, I'll just say that there are not many types of sexual encounters that I have not experienced at least once in my life. The more self-consumed I became, the more curious I became. I'm sure this will cause some readers to wonder what I'm talking about, but I'll leave it to your imagination. Whatever you're thinking, I've probably "been there and done that."

Does sharing my life and experiences make me vulnerable to attacks and scrutiny from others? Absolutely! But I decided a long time ago that my life is not my own. I'm now prepared for whatever may come of these revelations because for me, if anything I've shared causes chains to be broken in anyone's life, it was all worth it. I want those who can relate to my story on any level to know that you are not alone. It's easy to feel alienated and ostracized when you feel that what you are dealing with or experiencing is unique to you.

I'm not trying to start any excess drama with my next statements, but I may and I'm comfortable with that. Black people can be some of the most critical and judgmental people on this planet, especially in reference to their own. Yes, I said that. Black people. And I can make these statements because I have a lifetime of experience with my people, black people. I'm sad to admit that I was overjoyed to move away from them (in Bartow, and Wadley, Georgia) because of their small-minded, narrow ways of thinking.

For example, blacks have a stereotypical view of manhood and what a black man should be. In my opinion, the conventional view in the black community has little to do with who the man actually is, but more to do with how he looks and acts. Black men are not free to be diverse without inevitably being ostracized by their own people. I like to people-watch. One of the most interesting places to watch black men act out their manufactured masculinity is in the black barbershop. It's exceedingly entertaining and interesting to witness. If you get the opportunity, you should take a peak around sometime!

Everyone appears to be what they think everyone else in the room wants them to be, well versed in sports and things that sound macho. Even in political conversations, we black men have to speak such that we don't appear to put too much emotion into it. For black men, many feelings are a sign of weakness. And the only universally acceptable feeling a black man can show in public is anger…so you come across as an aggressive, alpha man's man. Even many of our women equate anger and aggression to masculinity, making statements like "I like when he gets aggressive with me and snatches me up." Yes, some of our women actually prefer abusive relationships. That's what they've been taught is associated with masculinity. What a wild theory right? Sadly, not so much in the black community.

Too many black men are forced to hide who they truly are for fear of isolation and rejection by their own people (as if rejection by the rest of the world isn't enough!). Truth be told, black men are not free to be honest and open about much. Many women say they want that from their man but how many would love him no matter what? There's been a lot of talk about how black men on the "down low" are hurting our black women. While there is some validity to this claim, many people speak on this subject out of biased ignorance.

Oftentimes, people with the greatest insecurities spend a lot of time inside their own heads, mulling through their own thoughts, rehearsing the things that produce their insecurities. I once heard someone say that his worst behaviors were produced from some of his darkest thoughts. That holds true for me, and I'm sure for many of you.

When our minds are not on Christ but on ourselves, the enemy can use our minds as his playground. Some of our thoughts, ideas and actions are produced from unresolved pains, insecurities and rejections, as if we have a need to return to the scene of the crime. In my case, while longing for my father I began to appreciate the admiration of other men. Confusion comes when those desires for male acceptance and the need for camaraderie, intermingle with sexual desire. You start to enjoy any kind word or admiring glance irrespective of the sex of the individual from whom it comes.

It takes you back to your childhood. Back to a place where, because you were not accepted, you attempt mentally to fill critical spaces left vacant. Back to a time that was filled with only rejection. We all want to be loved. We all want to be desired. All of us have an inner child, and many of our inner children have been through a great deal. However, we have not had the opportunity, through the many, nuanced paths we took, to deal with every issue that that our inner child has encountered.

So, what do we do? As we become adults, we feel that we have to push that inner child off into a corner like a scolded third grader that has been told by the teacher several times to be quiet. We may tell that little boy or girl to turn around and face the wall. And we leave them there for years so that only in quiet moments, moments of clarity, moments of reflection, do we allow for that child to turn around and say, simply, "May I have a moment to speak with you, please?"

Depending upon how painful, how deeply disruptive the situations that child causes us to rehash are, we may say, "No, turn back around and face the wall," thereby never truly dealing with any of the inner hurts and discouragement the inner child holds deeply within himself as he (or she) stares off into a dark and bleak corner. We're willing to tell that child: I know you're there, but I don't want to see your face right now. I don't want to have to deal with you in my current space. Sometimes it's easier (for us as adults) to keep things out of sight in order also to keep them out of mind. But this is avoidance of the inner issues. Where is the healing for that child? When can he or she turn around and have a conversation with you?

The little boy inside a man is capable of wreaking havoc on adult relationships. This proved true for me and my young marriage. Because of my insecurities, I was not able to engage or fully commit to my then wife, less so physically, but more so emotionally and mentally.

So, before you say, "I do," make sure you can. That sounds simple enough, but in reality, it's very profound. If you struggle with loving yourself, you will inevitably struggle with loving someone else. And over time, your lack of engagement with the ones that you say you love will likely start to wear on them physically, emotionally and mentally. This may even cause them to act out of character in response to what they are receiving from you. This also proved true in my marriage. The bonds of matrimony were broken on both of our parts through the very destructive forces of insecurities followed by infidelities. Ironically, sometimes the people who seem the most emotionally and mentally strong are the ones that have the deepest insecurities. Hurt people, hurt people.

Some may wonder if I'd ever marry again. In short, yes. I truly believe in the institution, and I believe that a God-ordained marriage is one of the greatest partnerships a human being can enter with another. However, it must be entered into with great caution, care and consideration. I know I'm not an easy person to love or be with. I have idiosyncrasies many people would find strange. But, I believe I'm definitely worth the effort. I think the good in me far outweighs all the rest, but that's just my opinion.

The late singer and actor Eartha Kitt once said, "I fall in love with myself and I want someone to share it with me." I find the phrasing a bit eccentric, but I understand the sentiment. I feel that two individuals first should have a profound love for themselves before entering into the union of marriage where you become one flesh. How can you passionately love someone else if you don't passionately love yourself? God teaches us to love others as ourselves; but what if we don't love ourselves? Then, we can't love others. The greatest gift you could ever give yourself is love.

Chapter Thought: Life can do one of two things to you: it can either teach you or beat you; the choice is yours. Self-discovery and self-love are two of the most vital components to living a life without limit. That's why it's so important to spend a considerable amount of time researching and falling in love with each component of yourself! When we give ourselves this gift, we essentially fill our emotional love banks up with unlimited currency to be poured out on whomever we choose. But when your bank is empty, you have nothing to offer.

When people attempt to withdraw from an empty love bank, one of two things happens: either someone goes into the red, or the transaction is denied. Either way, one of you walks away disappointed. That's why it's so critical to work on you first! Take your time and wait on the Lord. Follow your instincts. You'll know when the time and person are right! Don't say "I do," until you can!

CHAPTER NINE

"I praise you because I am fearfully and wonderfully made; your works are wonderful, I know that full well." Psalm 139:14 (NIV)

~The Introvert~

Because I love people so much, many people may find it hard to believe that I am introverted, but I adore showing my love for others. Working as a registered nurse at times requires a lot of person-to-person interaction, which is fine for me in the work place, but in my personal life, I prefer to be alone more often than not. An introvert is a person who gathers strength from long periods of time alone. Unlike extroverts, introverts don't need to be around a lot of people to be reenergized. Yet many of us work in jobs that call for us to be around or in front of many people daily. This can cause a great deal of confusion for those who have to deal with us.

I think my introversion stems from a lifetime of being alone. I was married for eleven years but quite often felt alone. It wasn't that my relationship was inadequate, but more so that I felt more strength and empowerment when I could retreat into my mind and think, alone. Being in a relationship with an introverted person is not easy for anyone, especially if the other individual is an extrovert.

Another anomaly about me is that although I have sung my entire life, and many know me for that reason, I've never truly enjoyed performing before people because I don't enjoy being scrutinized. Having struggled with insecurity means getting on a stage to be judged by an audience was never something that I relished. Later on, I came to realize and accept that I was never going to be a famous singer or gospel artist, as it was really not in my heart to do. However, I've found new joy in speaking words of encouragement to others. This is where I belong. It's a beautiful thing to discover your purpose. Do you know your purpose?

Chapter Thought: It's ok to be who God created you to be! Don't apologize to anyone for that!

CHAPTER TEN

"But he gives more grace. Therefore, it says, 'God opposes the proud but gives grace to the humble.'"
James 4:6 (ESV)

~No Seat at the President's Table~

God has blessed me greatly with a successful career in nursing. I've had many jobs but none more rewarding than my job as director of nursing in skilled nursing facilities. One day, while working as director of nursing in a skilled nursing facility in Lawrenceville, Georgia, our company's president came for a visit. He hadn't been to this location in over six years, but wanted to recognize us for the superior results from our annual survey. We'd been without a single deficiency, which in long-term care, is a big deal. So, you ask, what exactly is a "survey?" Skilled nursing homes participating in Medicare and Medicaid are required by law to undergo an annual survey and certification process conducted by the state's health department. Skilled nursing facilities must comply with Medicare and Medicaid guidelines as well as state law to continue to operate.

The survey process determines whether the quality of care, as intended by the state, is being provided within that skilled nursing facility. If a skilled nursing facility is found to have violated regulations, federal law enforcement options include denying payment for new admissions, fining the home, revoking Medicaid and Medicare certifications, or even closing the facility.

The reason this is so significant is that during this facility's previous survey, the place received several "immediate jeopardy" citations (one of the worst types of citations). These citations carry hefty fines as well as a stigma within the community. They make it look as though your facility is very poorly run by whomever is in leadership at the time of that survey. Ultimately, the company may let both the director of nursing (DON) and the executive director (ED) go due to the poor survey outcome. The survey in which this skilled nursing facility received several "immediate jeopardy" citations, was devastating for this facility, and both the ED and DON were terminated.

Soon after their terminations, I was hired along with an interim ED. We were commissioned with getting this nursing home back to its former glory. Through much prayer and hard work, God saw fit to allow us to have not only a great survey, but one in which there were no deficient practices, quite a comeback. No one could believe it. Many thought that there was no way we could receive such a prestigious acknowledgment on the heels of probably the worst survey this facility had ever had. This afforded us the opportunity to be graced with the presence of our company president.

So, there we were, the day of the president's visit. Everyone was overjoyed as he arrived. He made his rounds and met with staff members. We were all very excited about the president's visit because we all loved and admired him greatly. The fact that he would even take the time to travel from Tennessee just to congratulate us was mind-boggling. However, it seemed to be turning into more of a "who's who" of divisional and regional staff, as corporate staff started to show up to greet the president, many of whom were not present during those grueling months that led up to our annual survey.

The company's president has to be one of the most humble and loving people I have ever encountered. The first time I heard this great man speak, I was almost reduced to tears. He has such an incredible way with words. I'm so grateful to have had the opportunity to work for a company that fears and serves the Lord. This leader is truly a man serving God's own heart, which made this day even more special for so many of us. However, not only was this day for us to celebrate with him, it was also the interim executive director's last day and the first day for the new ED.

Naturally, much of the praise and accolades went to the interim ED for an excellent survey. They were well deserved. However, I was keenly aware of just how much work my clinical team had put into making that survey a success. But no one was acknowledging that. The lead executives acknowledged one another along with the interim ED and the incoming ED. All the while I sat in the back, just out of sight, knowing in my heart that the survey was largely due to the hard work of my department. I became a bit torn and momentarily disheartened. I didn't realize it at the time, but I was allowing pride to rear its ugly head in my heart at that moment. I once heard Dr. Rick Rigsby, a best-selling author and award-winning journalist say that "pride is the burden of a foolish person." There I was, being that foolish person. Satan was having a field day with my pride. All that played over and over again in my head was the fact that eighty percent of the survey related to things in my department. But that went unacknowledged.

Surveys usually run three to four days in length. Our survey took four days, and every single day I spent time building relationships with and answering questions for each of the surveyors. It was the nursing department and I that carried that survey through to victory, not corporate oversight.

So, during the scheduled "Presidents Lunch", there was a table set for the president, along with seats for whomever else was selected to sit with the president. While helping out in the dining area by straightening up the tablecloths for residents and staff, I overheard one of the regional staff members telling the food service director who would be sitting at the president's table. After he had gone down the list of corporate officials, my name was called after some prompting from the food service director, rather like an afterthought. He said, "Oh, yeah, Troy, you should eat with us too, buddy."

I smiled, nodded and kept working. I started to feel more and more bothered by this. I realized that I needed to do something to breakup and dismiss these thoughts. At first, I didn't know what to do. Then I heard in my heart, "Serve all of them their lunch." If you ever want to shut the mouth of pride and anger, serve! The enemy doesn't know what to do with that!

As the corporate staff entered the dining room following the president, they filed into seats at his table, one by one. Each seat was filled. I then walked over to the cart where the director of food service had placed each plate, and I started to serve each of them. Once I was done, I prepared my own plate, but there was no seat left at the president's table. There was, however, a smaller table just behind his with one other person sitting there, so I joined them. Moments later they asked the president to bless the food, so I walked over and kneeled down next to the seated guests as the president offered a wonderful prayer. After the prayer, I returned to my seat.

While I don't usually remain too concerned about this sort of thing throughout my day, this bothered me because it seemed that so many others were taking credit for what God had allowed my team to accomplish. It wasn't until I was on my way home that I heard the Lord say (and I'm paraphrasing here), "Whom did you do it for? Me or them?" I broke out in tears and prayed, "Father, forgive me!" I was reminded that everything we do, we should do as unto God, not seeking the approval or praise of any man! I then realized how selfish, prideful, and self-serving I had been. I immediately repented.

This moment of spiritual clarity made me grateful. I lifted my voice and said, "Thank you, Lord, for revealing me to me. Thank you for reminding me of whom I serve!" This was a new lesson for me, and I am both grateful and humbled by it.

Chapter Thought: Remember for whom you're doing things! Colossians 3:23 says, "Work willingly at whatever you do, as though you were working for the Lord rather than for people. Let your only desire be that God is glorified in you!" Many of us never get to the next level in Him because we can't shake the idea that it's not about us. So, stagnate you stay! Let's all work to get over ourselves! It's all about our heavenly Father! Can he truly use you?

CHAPTER ELEVEN

Wisdom is the principal thing; therefore, get wisdom: and with all thy getting get understanding. Proverbs 4:7 (KJV)

~What I've Learned~

Out of all the things I've experienced, I'm grateful to say that nothing has been wasted. From every trial, every circumstance, every situation, every embarrassment, God has been able to take the ashes of it and create something beautiful. Through it all, I've learned to love myself, and I've learned to love others. I've learned to cherish the moments spent with those who love me. I learned that I need God every single day of my life. I've learned that no matter how difficult life gets, no matter how dark it may seem or lonely I feel, God is always with me! His word promised He'd never leave me! I've learned that you can't buy love no matter what you use for currency. Some pay with money, but others pay with time, attention, affection or devotion.

I've learned that you don't get to where you want to go by staying where you are. You've got to keep moving. I've learned to be a car and not a train. Let me explain what I mean. Tracks guide trains, but cars make their own tracks. In other words, you don't have to go along with every situation you're in "just because." I've learned to make my own tracks. Without tracks trains don't work too well, but a car can function on virtually any terrain. I've learned not to make short-term decisions that may have long-term effects.

I've learned that the Potter doesn't mind my broken pieces. In fact, He prefers me that way! What potter wants an already completed work? Where is the artistry in that if the work has already been created, interpreted and put together? What the Potter wants is to take that work of art, already created, crush it to dust, add a little bit of living water to it and slap it on His potter's wheel as a new lump of clay. Only then does that potter have something with which to work. The Potter can re-define, re-interpret and/or recreate a new work of art from what was previously defined. Don't despise your broken pieces. Give them to the Potter. He'll make a masterpiece out of you!

I've learned that we overcome by the blood of Jesus Christ and the word of our testimony (Revelation 12:11), which is why I've shared some of my testimony in this book. I've learned to be like those punching balloons we used to play with as children. You punch with all your might, and yes, they fall over, but inevitably they pop back up. Why? Because they were not designed to be knocked down and stay down. Neither were you. Come what may, get back up again! Remember this, life is not ultimately about how you started... it's how you finish!

Made in the USA
Columbia, SC
04 February 2019